Majoring In Fatherhood

Calvin Crosby IV

Calvin Crosby IV

Copyright © 2018 Calvin Crosby IV
All rights reserved.
ISBN: 0-99-758513-1

DEDICATION

I would like to dedicate this book to my father who taught me how to be a father. My mother who was also my teacher. I especially want to dedicate this book to my children and the mothers of my children. If it was not for you guys I would not be a father. Thank you for giving me the gift of fatherhood.

And to the mother of my second son for giving me the extra push and inspiration to write this book.

Calvin Crosby IV

CONTENTS

INTRODUCTION	7
Freshman	**12**
The Possibility	13
Finding Out Your a Dad	20
Calvin Crosby III	27
To The Mothers of my kids	39
Sophomore	**42**
Parenting is not 50/50	43
Building a Bond	50
Having Children that you cannot Support	56
College Dad	60
Junior	**65**
Incarcerated Father	66
Lifetime Commitment	72
A Bullying Mother	77
Child Support	82
Senior	**91**
No Excuses	92
Breaking up with the Mother and not the Child	97
Father's Day	99
Finals	**102**
Truth or Slander	103
End of the Semester	**106**
The Final	107
Graduation Day	110

Calvin Crosby IV

INTRODUCTION

I decided to write this book because there is a shortage of actual father figures. For a long time, I could not understand how there is an overwhelming number of children claiming that they have a mother, but no father. This should not be happening and my job is to help change that and empower fathers to become more active in their children's lives.

As I was doing my research on books for fathers, I noticed that there were a lot of books on first time dads or books on how to be a father from a christian standpoint. I wanted to write a book on the reality of fatherhood and not fatherhood from a perfect world point of view. The reality is we are in a day and time where we are in blended families and the chances of someone having a child with someone whom they are not married to is high. There is not a lot of books that talks about blended families and, lets just call it what it is, baby mamas and baby daddies. When I was growing up artist would rap and sing songs about how they want a wifey or asking someone to be there wifey. In this day and time artists are now saying how they looking for a baby mama or who "gone be my baby mama tonight". Times have changed and I am just speaking reality in this book.

We probably can agree that the media and society have given fathers a negative image and reputation that we, as fathers, arguably have earned. We also can probably agree that some fathers believe that they are doing a great job but, in reality they are not. And though this is understandable, because I was once a father who believed to be doing a great job, in reality we're not even doing the minimum for our children.

In some cases, fathers simply do not know how to be a father, and that is ok too as this book is to help teach you how to be a father. Understand that no one, including myself, can teach you everything on being a father as some things are better learned through experience. The things that are shared throughout this book are my personal thoughts, views, and experiences. There is no perfect formula to being a father but I am simply giving you the tools to be a successful father. I also need you to understand that I am not a lawyer therefore I am not giving any legal advice throughout this book. If you are having legal trouble in regards to your child I strongly suggest that you seek legal advice and services from an attorney.

Upon purchasing this book, you have become my student and you are now seeking to major in fatherhood. By the end of this course, hopefully you will have all the resources and skills that will prepare you to graduate with your bachelors in fatherhood. Even if you have already majored in fatherhood look at this as a refresher course to stay up to date on your craft. This book is not only for fathers or anyone who is looking to become a father, but this book can also be for mothers or anyone who is helping to raise and teach a young man on how to be father. Think of this work as a bible or study guide throughout your journey of fatherhood.

I personally would like my readers to know that I am not a perfect man nor a perfect father and I make mistakes as well. Especially after my brief stint of being a "public figure" (I will explain this later in detail) it appears that the bar has been raised for me because of how TV portrays me as a perfect father and family man. Regardless, if it was my media appearances or my personal brand, I want you to know that I am not perfect and I hope that after reading this I have not disappointed you. If I have disappointed or hurt you after reading this book then I hope that you can forgive me and learn from my mistakes. I strive everyday to be a better man and live a lifestyle that is aligned with God, but if you have ever had an encounter with the devil then you know that the enemy is working and sometimes he tries to stop you from being great. Despite my downfalls there is a calling on my life that I must pursue and I must continue to pursue it despite the mistakes that I have made. I want you to know that lust, temptation, and the things of this world is real and if you are not rooted in God it will be very hard to overcome. I have written a book about fatherhood and provided uplifting insight in regards to fatherhood and I appreciate you for being so generous to support the cause and being humble enough to receive the information that I have to offer you in regards to fatherhood.

Majoring In Fatherhood

Freshman

1
THE POSSIBILITY

As a male, growing up we have high aspirations of being a dad and being the best dad to our unborn child. We pretty much have our whole fatherhood life planned out way before the child is born, especially when expecting a boy. Do not get me wrong we have big plans for our daughters as well; moments such as walking them down the aisle, being their first love, and all the other amazing things that comes with being a father to our daughters. Nevertheless there is just another level of excitement when you know that you will become a father to a son. If you go back in history, certain religious groups and cultures took pride and rejoiced when there was a birth of a male. Birthing a male could be a huge advantage to your family and

family legacy especially in a male dominant culture.
First let's talk about the Bible and its history of birthing a son. Most of us may be familiar with the story of Jacob, found in Genesis chapter 29. Jacob looked upon a woman name Rachel and believed she was beautiful. Jacob loved Rachel so much that he wanted to marry her. Keep in mind Rachel had a sister name Leah. The Bible stated that Leah was "tender eyed" but Rachel was beautiful with a nice figure. Jacob asked Rachel's father if he could serve him for seven years and in return he would give him Rachel as his wife. Rachel's father accepted the offer of Jacob and Jacob served him for seven years. After Jacob had served him for seven years he asked Rachel's father to bring him his wife Rachel so that he may have sex with her. When Jacob woke up in the morning he saw that Rachel's father had brought him Leah and not Rachel. The father stated if you serve me another seven years I will give you my daughter Rachel. Jacob served another seven years and in return received Rachel as his wife as well. The Bible tells us he loved Rachel more than he loved Leah. This story helps us point out to you the joy of wanting to be a dad, a woman wanting the opportunity to make someone a dad, and just being a parent in general. The Bible tells us that the Lord saw that Leah was hated so he opened her womb so that she can conceive, but Rachel was barren and could not conceive. Leah was pregnant and gave birth to a SON! Leah believed that the Lord blessed her

and removed her affliction of not being able to give birth and allowed her to birth a son. In this time being able to give birth especially to a son was a huge blessing. In fact if you could not have kids you were ashamed and almost considered useless especially to a man. This is why Leah said the Lord blessed her and in that same sentence she stated now my husband will love me. Pretty sad, huh?

It gets better for Leah though; Leah went from not being able to have kids and when it was all said and done she ended up giving Jacob six sons. After all that she stated how she must praise the Lord cause the Lord saw how she was hated by her husband Jacob and now she is important to Jacob because she gave him six sons. As you can see even in the Bible it was a blessing to be a father and, in particular, a father to a son. Leah was not only favored because she was able to give birth, but in addition to giving birth she was able to give birth to six boys.

We can also talk about Sarah and her issue with not being able to give birth. Sarah desired so badly to give her husband, Abraham, a child that she allowed her maid to be his wife so that she may conceive a child for Abraham. As you may know, the maid conceived a son and his name was Ishmael. Eventually the Lord found favor in Sarah and allowed her to conceive a son and his name was Isaac.

As fathers we all have these great visions and

dreams on how our life will be as a dad, similar to the people we just spoke about. Then BOOM, you find out she is pregnant and you think all those dreams are out the window. In some cases, some fathers may feel like everything has changed, but in other cases some believe their fatherhood is off to a great start and going as planned.

For the dads who are starting off on the right track, your introduction to fatherhood probably looks similar to something like this:

You get married and then have a child with your wife. If this is you, congratulations on your awesome start of fatherhood. If this is not you, well, let's just say you are in for a ride during your journey into fatherhood. I can almost bet that ninety percent of males have the vision of being married before having a child. Which is a smart plan to have because it will save you a ton of headaches. For the ones who did not start off this way, just know it is not too late to get back on track and Major in Fatherhood.

For those who did not have a child with their wife, it probably looked similar to something like this:

You got someone pregnant and it could be your girlfriend or someone you were just messing around with. The first problem that you have just encountered is having a baby with someone that you may not spend the rest of your life with. If you plan to be with that person for the rest of your life and it ends up happening that way then good, but if not then continue to follow me. So now you are about to have a baby with someone whom you do not plan to be with for the rest of your life. What you have just told me is that your child is likely going to grow up with step parents and in a blended family. This alone can cause a whole lot of problems. A child growing up in a blended family cannot only cause harm to the parents, but it can also cause harm to the child. I was fortunate enough to not experience that as a child, but I am experiencing it through my kids and as a parent.

Outside of having to work through blended families, one could encounter fighting to contribute to your child's name. In marriages, deciding on a baby name could be something that the parents may not agree on but they likely will not turn it into a problem. A married couple can normally come to an agreement as opposed to a non-married couple. One thing for sure the last name will never be an issue for a married couple. I cannot say the same for non-married couples as in some cases I have witnessed the mother not giving the father's last name to the child. In most cases, when I have observed this it was based on the father's actions such as being absent during the pregnancy or proving to the mother that he will be absent throughout the child's life. Regardless of the fact if this is you, you can always get legal advice and take legal action. The easiest thing to do is to prove yourself responsible and be a responsible father so that this issue may be avoided.

Another issue you may encounter is abortion. Whether the abortion is something you want, she wants, or a mutual agreement either way having an abortion is not a fun ride. Let's say that you want to abort the baby but she does not. Understand that this will be a very difficult conversation to have with a woman, and in particular the woman of your child. Asking her to abort the baby could possibly damage her forever. She now knows that you do not want to have a baby with her when she probably was excited to have one. Regardless if she wanted the baby or not you have just asked her to kill her baby for your own personal reasons. If she decides to have that baby she will remember for the rest of her life that you wanted to have that baby aborted. This can scar her and she will reference this later.

There could also be the scenario where you want the baby but she does not want the baby. What do you do then? Well there is not much you can do in this situation because she can pretty much have the abortion without your permission. So she just crushed your dreams of having a child, for now at least. Let's say that aborting the baby is a mutual decision. This will still be a tough journey to take, and if you decide to take this journey I want to help prepare you for this journey. When a woman is having an abortion this can be a very sad time for her, short term and long term. Long term, every year around the time of the abortion she will say to herself "my child would have been this age if I would have kept the baby". She may even start living with regrets. Short term will be the emotional trauma that she have to face with aborting her baby and the pain that she will endure during the process. As a father it is your job to be there for her in this time of need. Even if you have to take a day off of work to be with her, do it, she will appreciate you for this. Whatever she decides to do just be sure that you are 100% supportive, because you have no idea what she will be going through mentally and emotionally. It is very unlikely that a married couple will have an abortion because most married couples plan to have a family and even if its an accident they can accept it more because they are married.

2

Finding Out Your a Dad

When I found out I was having my first son it was a very horrible experience, again no disrespect to the mother but, she would probably agree that it was a horrible experience for the both of us. I remember pretty vividly finding out I was going to be a dad. I remember the mother telling me before she even took the test that she was pregnant. Of course I was like "girl you not pregnant your period just coming late"; my arrogance led me to believe that my pull out game was too strong to get anyone pregnant. Plus, some females always think they pregnant when they cycle comes late. Their cycle will be a whole two minutes late and they hollering they pregnant. So I was like "girl you are not pregnant" but she insisted that she was pregnant and stated that she knows she is pregnant because of the changes within her body. Well, she was right, she was not even a whole month pregnant when she guessed that she was pregnant and sure enough she was right. I remember getting that text from her saying she was pregnant, and me replying back "ok". What an idiot, yes I know. And by no means am I proud of this but again just sharing my story so that others can see I graduated and was able to overcome my shortcomings. After my short response, she asked "what are we going to do about this", and I sent another dumb text along the lines saying "what you mean what we going to do, we are going to have a baby." Obviously coming off in a sarcastic way because I knew what she was trying to ask me. She wanted to know future plans since we have to plan for a baby now, but I was just not ready to be a father at that time. I was twenty-one, in college getting ready to have my first child, and just wanted to live the best years of my college life. I just simply wanted to continue to party and be with other women, that's not too much for a young man like myself to ask for, was it? I did not want to be tied down to the responsibility of having to take care of a child. I was also extremely selfish at the time and just wanted to spend my money on me and the things that I desired of this world; definitely not spending it on diapers and baby needs.

Throughout the whole pregnancy I was in denial, and even had thoughts on what if my baby did not make it and how I would be ok with that. I never asked for an abortion because I knew that she was not going to have that, and it would have did nothing but piss her off. I was smart enough to pick and choose my battles and I knew that was not a battle I wanted to fight. I do recall her saying things to try and trigger me, but I tried my best to keep my cool. It did not work all the time but I tried my best to not allow her to get the best of me. I recall one time she sent me a text message saying that she was thinking about having an abortion. She mentioned that she can tell I did not want the baby and she did not want to have a baby with someone she was not married to. I was not going for that trap, I just simply stated "ok you can do what you like". Then of course, it turned into a big argument anyway. She made comments such as "oh you will be ok with that" or "well I need to react fast cause time is running short". We both know that she was not thinking about no abortion and she was just seeking attention from me in which I understood. . After all, she was pregnant and I was not acknowledging her pregnancy as a upstanding father should. I also believe that she wanted to have the baby because she believed that it was a way to slow me down and be committed to her. I could be wrong but this is how I saw things from my perspective. I believed at that time she wanted to slow me down and still to this day I believe that those were her intentions.

Since our split, she has not treated or reacted to guys

that have put her in similar situations the way she reacted to me. Which furthermore has me to believe that she was hoping to tie me down. Let me address something before we move on, she is over me and has since moved on with other relationships. Furthermore, I am not stating she still wants to be with me and trying to tie me down, that is not what I am saying at all. In fact she probably cannot stand me now and even regrets having a son with me. that is also not to say that she thinks I am a horrible dad either but you get my point. Another one she tried to pull on me was informing me that she was not giving the baby my last name. Now that statement did work on me and I was furious. I still remember going to class and taking it out on other students on campus. She told me that since we were not married she did not want to have a different last name from her child. I was pissed and just did not understand why she would do this to me. Why she would not let me build on my legacy especially if it was a boy. I also did not mind not naming him Calvin Crosby V because we were not married and I was unsure on what the future held for me, my son, and my legacy. Not only my legacy but the Crosby legacy. On the other hand, I was also afraid that what if I never have another son. If I did not have another son the Crosby legacy would be ruined and come to an end. It was something that I was surely concerned and torn about. I never pressured her in naming the baby after me, but I did dispute the fact that she did not want to give the baby my last name. As time went on and the relationship became more positive throughout the pregnancy, I did ask her what did she plan to name the baby and she looked at me and said "duh I am going to name him Calvin Crosby V". I did not suggest that name to her nor did I pressure her in any kind of way. I can appreciate her for that and I believe that says a lot about the legacy of Crosby men and in particular my great-grandfather, grandfather, and father. She knew that my son was in good hands and to be named after these fine gentlemen was nothing short of an honor. If they were not good man and wonderful fathers then the situation may have ended up a little different.

Deadbeat Fathers Session X

Let's pause and switch gears for a second in regards to naming a child after you. Nothing irks me more than a no good father wanting to name his son after him. That is very prideful, selfish, and just plain sorry to me. You are saying you want to have a little junior but yet you are not taking care of the little junior. What kind of legacy is that to leave? You are being so selfish and concerned about your name and wanting to start a "legacy" that you are so desperately willing to name your son after you but you will not even be around to set a GOOD example of what being a father is and what it means to carry out your name and your legacy. I'm not just talking about no every other weekend type of dad or being a dad when it is only convenient for you, but I am talking about a dad who is thoroughly immersed in the child's life. We will discuss in more details on what it is to be a good dad and what I mean by an every other weekend dad in later sections. The next problem I had or more like she had was living arrangement. I was not about to leave college just to be with her and the baby. I know that was something she wanted me to do, but again I wanted to stay in college living the college life and not bear the full responsibility of being a dad. My mom had already agreed to take care of the baby while I was in school and she can go back to school or do whatever it was she believes is needed for her to establish herself as we introduce life to a child that obviously needed financial support. I had no shame in letting my mother temporarily take on most of the burden of taking care of my child while I was in school. For one I was not the first nor will be the last person to let their parent take care of a child while completing school. Secondly, I had a bigger purpose in completing school because I knew I had a child that would be depending on me. I knew that it would be hard for me to raise my child without an education. The end results was that the mother and baby moved in with my parents and then a few months later they moved in with me.

Another problem that you may encounter which is technically not a "problem", but can just simply be another thing to deal with and that is child support. I say it is not a problem because at the end of the day that is your child and the money is supposed to be used to take care of your child, so technically it should not be a problem but sometimes it can be. I discuss more about child support in the section titled "Child Support". You want to know something else that you may run into when having a baby outside of marriage? Having a "baby mama", that's right I used the word baby mama. You can surely avoid having a baby mama if you do not get anyone pregnant that is not your wife. A lot of people do not like to the term baby mama because I guess it has a negative connotation. Well the truth of the matter is do not get someone pregnant that is not your wife and you will not have to worry about having a "baby mama" or as some may say "baby mama drama". Remember all these problems can be avoided if you do it the right way and wait until you are married to have a child. Nevertheless, on September 10, 2011 my life was changed forever as I was introduced to fatherhood by a young man name Calvin Crosby V.

3

CALVIN CROSBY III

They say you appreciate your parents more when you become a parent and with my newly found parenthood I find this to be true. Things that I did not appreciate before, I can appreciate now and if it was not for my father I would not be the man or father that I am today. I think you guys missed that, it took a father to make me a great father. If you have not majored in fatherhood then what makes you think we will have more scholarly fathers? Or that you can help your son be a scholarly father? If you did not get that you will probably understand it more at the end of this book.

I strive to be a great father like my dad but he tells me that I am already a better father than he was. *I don't believe that for one second.* Growing up I did not want to take the same path in life as my father. People would tell me how I would take on his church when he passed. At the time I did not want anything to do with my father's church or being in church for that matter (yes I was a pastor kid and yes I know I did not act like one). My mother would say "you should go do this like your father" or "be like this like your father" and I hated it! Especially when they would talk to me about taking on his church. I wanted to be my own man and take on a different path in life. Though I did not want to take on the same path as my father, I definitely wanted to be an outstanding father and husband like he was. Of course I failed at both and sometimes I beat myself up about it because I am not like him. My father always tells me that it is ok and how I am doing a good job. Being a father and a man myself I can be less receptive towards it because I feel like he is just doing what a good father is supposed to do and that is keeping me encouraged. What I love most about my father is that he took really good care of his wife which is my mom, and he was a very active and outstanding father in me and my sister's life. My father did what was needed to keep his marriage and family together, and for that I can respect him because I know through experience it is hard to keep a family together. Unfortunately for me I did not keep mines together and that is why I am not a better father than my dad. My father played many roles throughout his life and I do not think he fell short in any of his roles. My father was a husband, student, pastor, son, brother, and of course a father. He played many other roles but these were probably his most important. My favorite role of my father is him being a pastor. When I was younger it was not my favorite and I actually hated him in that role. As a pastor kid I was forced to go to church and it can be quite embarrassing when you are the only one who has to go to church. Or while my friends are sleeping in I am the only one who is waking up early to go to church. As I look back now I am very thankful and appreciative for both my father and mother for making me go to church and raising me up with Christian principles. In fact, I regret while living with my parents I was not absorbing and receiving all that spiritual knowledge and helping my father build his ministry to change lives and please our heavenly father which is our Lord and savior Jesus Christ. That is one of the biggest regret I have and that is not taking advantage of the spiritual and non-spiritual guidance that I was living under for so many years. My next favorite role from my father is him being a husband and a strong family man. As I am continuing to grow to be a family man and father, I know that this is not an easy task. I have never witnessed any man take care of his wife the way my father takes care of my mother. I can only wish to be as a great of a husband as my dad has been to my mom. I know to be great like that it takes a lot of prayer and patience. Trust me I am working on both of that right now. This might sound kind of whack of me but I was never really the kid who said they will have multiple woman growing up or made comments like I'm not ever getting married. I admired my parents marriage so much that I said to myself I want to be a part of something like that when I get older. As a father and a man, often times we let our frustration take over our better judgement and because of this it is hard to accomplish what my father did. Which is having one wife, two kids, no outside kids, and being married for thirty years and counting. As fathers we must use our better judgement and know when it is necessary to fight and keep our family together. Beyond that we must take the appropriate measures and steps to keep our family together as well. That is something my father did and unfortunately I did not and that is why I say I can never be like my father. There was a research conducted and it stated that people like me are rare. Meaning if you live in the home with both your parents and they are married, then consider yourself lucky and rare. After hearing about that research and being told over the years by family and friends, I began to really appreciate that at a young age. My cousins would joke about how proper I talk because I would say something like "I have to ask my parents". They would reply back by saying why do you talk so proper. They would then turn around and say well maybe it just sounds proper to us because we are not used to saying or hearing the word parents. My friends and family would always tell me to look around as I am the only one whose father is around. I know a huge part of this was the effort from both my father and mother fighting to keep the family together, and for that I thank them both for their hard work. Speaking of being rare and my cousins making jokes of me being proper I am reminded of a time when I saw D.L Hughley stand up. He made a joke about Michael Jackson's book and stated how Michael mentioned he wanted to live a regular life with a regular family. In particular he mentioned the relationship with him and his father and how is father did not love him. Of course D.L Hughley made this joke funny by adding his commentary to it, but one thing he mentioned was that Michael did not want a normal dad. D.L Hughley stated that normal dads have outside kids, and sometimes the kids do not know until the funeral. He stated the kids will be at the funeral talking about who is that and why they look like daddy. To add to D.L Hughley joke the next thing the kids would have to worry about after his funeral is fighting of the father estate because he has outside kids. I have personally witnessed this happen and going to court over these things are not pretty. Of course this is not true about all fathers but it is not uncommon for a father to have outside kids or have kids with more than one mother. To D.L Hughley's point Michael had a good father who was involved in all his kids life, he was not in a blended family, was able to grow up in a home with both his mother and father, and Michael's father helped his son reach fame and fortune by becoming a successful recording artist. My point in using D.L Hughley's jokes is to point out that though he was making jokes about fathers, some of his jokes were true, and as fathers we need to change society perception of fathers so the next time D.L Hughley decides to make a joke about fathers he can say that Michael wanted a normal father.

One of my favorite memories of my father is when he went back to school at the University of Texas at Arlington. At the time I did not realize how significant it was but as I look back at it now I see that it was a huge deal that my father went back to school and received a college degree. I can recall being in middle school and sitting at the table doing homework, and sitting next to me would be my sister working on her homework, and my dad working on his homework. At the time I'm thinking my dad is too old to be having homework, and he may have been but that is what happens when you decide to pursue a degree later in life. Nevertheless, he completed school and received his bachelor's degree in Social Work. Due to him going back and receiving his degree it allowed him to set the standards for me. Being a college graduate allowed my father to practice what he preached and he was able to set a higher standard for me because as parents we always tell our kids to be better than me. So I guess one of the ways I could be better than him his by furthering my education. So it left me no choice but to pursue and receive my masters degree. With that being said I guess my children have to be better than me and pursue a PhD ha! But seriously I would never have expectations for my children to receive a PhD, but what I do expect is for my sons to be successful in whatever career choice they pursue and to receive some type of education. My father graduating from college also allowed me to witness the growth and benefit of receiving an education. After my father received an education he was able to move our family in a better neighborhood, we began to take really nice family trips out of the country, went from having one family car to my parents each having a car of their choice, and the list just continued to grow on the amount of blessings my dad received after receiving an education. One thing for sure my dad would emphasize on is that none of this would be possible without the guidance of God, and to be clear on which God we are referring to we are talking about Jesus Christ! That is the God my father give all thanks to for making any of this possible.

One thing that my father did that I can respect him the most for and that is keeping his family together. As men and women we know that this is a very hard task to do. I failed to keep my family together with my first son, but regardless if I was able to keep my family together or not I will always be a father to my son and I want to make sure that you do the same. I am very honored and thankful that my father kept his family together and allowed me to grow up in a functional family with only one mother, one father, and no outside kids. I put so much morals and values to family and a lot of this has to do with the way my parents raised me and how they value family. People would make jokes of us and tell us that we are like a sitcom family, similar to the Huxtables because of the way my family operated. If you are reading this ask yourself did you keep your family together. If not, then ask yourself is it too late to bring your family together. If it is not to late and you do attempt to bring your family back together ask yourself another question, will it be healthy for the family as a whole to be together. Having the family together may not be in the best interest of the family. In most cases I can almost guarantee it is in the best interest of the family, but in very few cases it may not be in the best interest of the family to be together. I can recall witnessing a family talk about their problems as a family, and how they mentioned they only stayed together for their daughter. Well, watch this ...... so the daughter stated how much she hated her father because he did not make her mother happy and that it just did not feel like a family nor did they function as a family. With the father effort in keeping his family together his daughter still managed to hate him in spite of him sacrificing his happiness in attempt to keep his daughter happy. In this case it may have been in the best interest for the parents to part ways because the daughter witnessed dysfunction within the family, she was not able to witness how a husband is supposed to treat his wife, and more importantly she witnessed her father making her mother unhappy which in return made her unhappy. What probably hurt her the most was that it was not just some random guy making her mother unhappy, but it was her father who was bringing the hurt to her mother. At the end of the day a child can oftentimes respect a man that makes their mother happy. This is why when you ask someone if they like their stepfather and their response is no, they often times follow it up with something along the lines like "I don't really care for him but he makes my mother happy and for that I like him". So as a father if you decide to bring your family back together, make sure that it will be healthy and you demonstrate to your kids how a family is supposed to look. If not, it may backfire on you and this may hinder you from majoring in fatherhood.

  I also cannot talk about my father and how he majored in being a father without talking about my mother. In my time of being a father I learned that you can be a great father without the support of the mother, but you can be an even greater father with the support of the mother. My father is probably half the father he is due to the support of my mother supporting him as a father. If you do not think a supportive mother supporting the father makes a difference ask yourself this. Have you ever met a father who have had several kids and was not a good father to his kids. Then all of a sudden that father has another child and is actively being the best father to that child. More than likely it was probably because of the support of that child's mother. The mother encouraged, supported, and held the father accountable of that child. Notice I did not say she forced him or left him with an alternative such as you better do this or I am going to do that, but she provided genuine and sincere uplift to the father. When the mother gets to a point where she is making demands and being aggressive to the father, she is practically bullying the father and at this point rarely does anything good comes out of bullying the father. Do not get me wrong in some cases the mother, grandparents, and everyone that is involved in the father's life have done what is needed to support the father but he still refuses to take on the responsibility of being a father. In this case your only option is to take legal action, but whatever you decide to do please do not beat yourself up over the situation or dwell on the fact that your child has an absent father. At the end of the day it is the father's choice on rather or not if he will step and be a father. Moms can really be hard on themselves for this but I read a meme and it said "do not stress over these guys not wanting to be in your baby's life because it is enough step daddy's out here." Funny meme but at the same time it is a true meme. There are a lot of males out there that love kids and cannot wait to step up and be the father to that fatherless child. Trust me I was an active father in my son's life and his mother and the boyfriend still tried to move me to the side and portray him as if he was the father to my son. I'm not saying that they went all out and was teaching him to stop calling me daddy, but to some degree they influenced my son to think that they were a family and he was my son's father and they were not married. Of course if they were married then that would be a different story but they were not, and I still remember her telling me that he is more of a male model to my son than I was. At the time it hurt but I am now confident to know my worth as a father so things like that do not hurt me. I have now learned to know my worth as a father and the things that both of the sons mother say to me no longer hurts. Of course I wish they would not say some of the hurtful things they say but I cannot control that. Ok I got in my soap box for a minute but let's get back to my mother and the important role she played in my father majoring in fatherhood. As mothers they have the tendency to be very micromanaging when it comes to their kids. Mothers believe they have to be in every decision making of the child's life and they pretty much get the last say. It is funny to me when the mother ask's for your opinion and then try and change your mind on the opinion or just ignore everything you have suggested. It is like why ask right? I learned earlier on you cannot win many battles against the mother when it comes to making decisions in regards to your children, and if you do win it was probably a blood bath. The decision making is an 80/20 effort with mothers being 80% in charge of the decision, and the finances is an 80/20 effort with the fathers having the 80% responsibility of the finances. As fathers we wish we had more of a say but for now we only make about 20% of the decisions in the child's life. Please do not take that statement literally or overthink it to much but I think you get my point. With that being said I must acknowledge my mother on sitting back and trusting my father to lead as a father and make tough decisions. This is very hard for a mother to do as they like to micromanage, but my mother humbled herself and trusted my father enough to lead. For that I thank my mother for allowing my father to learn and teach to his full potential of being a father, and because of that it has allowed me to learn from him and be the father that I am today. Mama I thank you for supporting me and daddy as we strive to become a better father and overall human being

4
TO THE MOTHERS OF MY KIDS

To the mother of my first son: I am sure you regret the day of being pregnant by me and even with the regrets I still want to thank you for being an outstanding mother to our son. It brings me joy to know the love you have for our son and the mother and son bond you two have. At one point of time I would tell myself that he was better off being with you than me, but could never fix my mouth to tell you that. Now that I have graduated and majored in fatherhood, I now have the dignity to say that. You may have also given me a hard time about a lot of things when it came down to our son, but those were learning moments for me and now I have the opportunity to take those moments and teach other fathers on how to first avoid those problems, and secondly handle those problems if they cannot be avoided. I appreciate you for giving me Calvin Crosby V as he has also taught me how to be a father and has helped me to receive my degree in fatherhood.

To the mother of my second son: I want to thank you for all that you have done for me. I appreciate you for being patient with me as a father and I pray that you continue to be patient with me as I continue to grow to be a better father and a better man overall. I want to thank you for giving me my second son as he is a true bundle of joy. I love that little man to pieces and I do not think no one understands how much love I have for that young man. He brings me a lot of joy and makes me proud to be a father. I hope that he does the same for you and your journey of motherhood.

To both of the mothers of my sons: I know that I have caused you both a great deal of pain as a father, but I want to take this moment to appreciate the both of you and for your patience with me as I continue to grow as a father. I know that having me as the father of your children is not an easy task, but I want to thank you both for allowing me to make mistakes and giving me time to learn from them. It is definitely not easy being a father and especially to a father of kids living in two different homes. You would not believe how hard it is to balance both homes, but just know every decision that I have made is based on what I believe is to be in the best interest of our children. Sometimes my decision may not have been the best decision but at the time I believed it to be the best decision and I can live with that. Understand that this book is not a personal attack on either one of you, but I am simply sharing my views, thoughts, and experience of the road to fatherhood and how to major in fatherhood. My hopes is to empower other fathers to step up and not make the same mistakes that I did as a father. You both should know that my heart is pure and I am writing this book with love as I love you both.

      To my scholars take note on what I just did. I praised and appreciated the mothers of my children as mothers. Woman in general love to be praised and complimented.

Sophomore

5

Parenting is not 50/50

Parenting is not always a 50/50 contribution from both parents. Sometimes your contribution may vary. As a father you must remember that your child is your responsibility despite what the mother is doing for the child. It is not fair to let your child suffer because you believe the mother should be contributing more. You must also keep in mind there will be times when the mother is carrying the bulk of the responsibility, and just like she was patient with you as she took on more responsibility, you must also be patient with her as you may take on more responsibility.

As a father there will surely be times that you may require the mother to take on a bulk of the responsibility. For myself, this happened when I went to college, graduate school, voluntarily spent 60 days in jail, and a whole list of other pivotal moments in my life. While partaking in all these endeavors I needed the support of their mothers. The time that I was using to invest in my goals, was time being taken away from my kids. In return, I needed their mother to step up and take on the bulk of the responsibility. A lot of my goals would have been extremely hard to complete without the support of their mothers. Just like there will be times the mother takes on more responsibilities, you too must reciprocate.

When requesting more help from the mother or trying to figure out how can you contribute more as a father, do not base it on a 50/50 scale. For starters it is hard to just only contribute 50 percent to your child. Not only is it hard but you should not want to limit yourself on the amount of time and money you invest in your child. There can never be to much time or money invested into your child. In fact you should be investing 110 percent of your effort into your child. Though you could never invest too much into your child, you want to be sure to invest your money and time wisely as well. I can rest assure you that if you do thy duty that is best and leave unto the lord the rest, you will never have that "50/50" talk with the mother.

When investing into your children you must not only invest into them when it is convenient for you, but you must also invest in them when it is also inconvenient for you as well. If you have not learned by now being a father is inconvenient and there is almost a never convenient time to be a father. What frustrates mothers the most is when the father only invest time and money when it is convenient for the father. I become very disappointed when I hear fathers come up with all these excuses on why they cannot do for their child and in reality they not doing what they should be doing for their child because they are putting self first, and to put their child first is an inconvenience. As a father sometimes you have to take off work, pick up a second job, and sacrifice your happiness for your child. This does not mean that you do not take care of yourself and do the things that you enjoy the most in life. As a father you must know how to take care of yourself because if you cannot take care of yourself how can you take care of a child who will be 100% depending on you. The key to assure that you are taking care of your child and yourself is finding that perfect balance between the two. For example, maybe one summer you do not invest to much money into your child by taking them to Disney World. Instead you take that few thousand dollars that you were going to spend at Disney World and take them to a few local theme parks, skating, bowling, and whatever else they like to do that is local and affordable. You take the rest of that money and you treat yourself to a trip to Las Vegas or whatever is you like to do for fun. Maybe the following year or so you sacrifice your personal trip and use that money to take them to Disney World or any other big vacation that you think they may like. That is how you balance the two and assure that you are making yourself and your children happy. To give you an example on a smaller level, sometimes you have to sacrifice buying clothes or going out to expensive restaurants and use those funds to invest in your child's education or extra curricular activities. It is not fair for you to treat yourself to the things you like to partake in on a day to day basis but your child is not a part of any club, sports team, or extra curricular activity. Be sure that your child is also partaking in things that they like to do on a day to day basis, this is how you can balance the two on a smaller level. What also disappoints me is when a father uses his child as an excuse on why they are not investing any time or money into their child. For example, when a father is off in college and stating that they are away in college so that they can prepare a future for their child. When in reality they are off to college doing everything but preparing a future for their child. It is ok to sacrifice being away from your child to build a better future for them such as joining the military or going off to college, as I was one of those fathers who went off to college, but do not use that as an excuse to run away from your responsibilities. Do what you need to do and come back and enjoy the fruits of your labors with your child. That is exactly what I did, I was able to finish school and provide a better life for my son. Be sure that you stick to your purpose and finish out that purpose so that you can pave the way for your children. Ask yourself this if you was to die today would you leave a positive legacy for your children. If not, we have work to do scholars and the work starts now.

Not being a "50/50" parent also means we are not standard visitation fathers. Let me repeat myself, fathers we are NOT standard visitation fathers. What I mean by standard visitation fathers is we are not fathers who only see our children every other weekend or on standard visitation that is set up by the courts, but we see our children just as much as the mothers do or if not close to as much as the mothers do. Your father may have been an every other weekend father but you will not be an every other weekend father. As I mentioned in this book it is important that we spend quality and meaningful time with our children. Spending time with your child every other weekend is not much quality time when there are 365 days out of the year. If you choose to only get your child every other weekend this means you are spending time with them roughly about two days every other week. That is lame scholar and that is not what fathers who major in fatherhood do. For one why would you want to put that burden on the mother to take responsibility of the child when he/she is not with you, and that is a lot of days and time that you are going without spending time with your child. Remember your child is an investment, invest as much time as you can into them and because great fathers make other great fathers. Also I do not want to be mistaken when I say that us fathers must spend time with our children outside of standard visitation. I know that there are a few cases when the mother will only allow for the father to have the child on the days that are ordered from the court and not a day more or a day less. In this case you just have to make best of the time that is allotted to you or request for more days with your child through the courts.

I do understand in this section I talk a lot about investing money and time into your children, but please do not make the mistake of thinking that the more money you invest into your children is a substitute of time that should be invested. Yes, there is no doubt kids love the money you invest into them but they also appreciate the time that is invested as well. The time will be more appreciated as they get older. I personally know people who have invested a lot of money into their children, but invested very little to no time and the overall relationship is not a very good relationship due to the lack of time being spent. This message particularly relates to fathers who have a daughter. It is so important that you invest that personal time with your daughter, as it is needed especially in today's society. As a teacher and individual who works with children on a daily basis, you would be surprised on how these young ladies think and how unaware they are of their worth. I have seen little Beyoncé's walking around my school out here chasing Suge Knights, when they should be out here chasing little Obama's. Unfortunately, this type of behavior can rollover to adulthood and your daughter is with a man that she has no business being with. Fathers, please invest valuable and meaningful minutes into your daughter.

6

BUILDING A BOND

No disrespect to the fathers as I am a father, but as fathers we will rarely be able to build a bond with our child like the mother can. It is not to say that we cannot build a bond as strong as the mother but it will be nothing like the mother nor will it be as quick as the mother. Before the child is even born the mother is already building a bond with the child. So you ask how can a mother build a bond with an unborn child? It is simple, as the child is growing in the belly of the mother she is building a bond. The moving, growing, and simple fact of knowing that there is another human inside one's body is enough for a mother to already have unconditional love and build that bond with the child before the child is even born. The Bible also has scriptures that refers to the bond and love a mother have for a child. In John 16:21 it states "a woman giving birth to a child has pain because her time has come, but when her baby is born she forgets the anguish because of her joy that a child is born into the world." Whatever problem or pain that mother has went through or is currently going through prior to giving birth, in that moment she forgets all her pain and sorrows because of the joy her child brings by being born into the world. In Isaiah 49:15 God makes a correlation between a mothers love for her infant child with his love for his children. The scripture states can a mother forget her child that she nurses? Can a mother fail to love a child that came from her own body or can she ever forget a child that came from her body? God was telling his people just like a mother that cannot forget her child that she is nursing, neither can God forget about his children. The bond of a mother and child is so strong that God makes reference to this when he compares how much he loves his children and how he will not forget about his children. Though mothers may have a head start when it comes to bonding with your children, this does not mean that you cannot get a head start on bonding with the child or create one as strong as the mother.

    As I mentioned earlier a mother quite naturally has a head start on building a bond but as fathers we can also get a head start on building a bond with our unborn child. One of the first things we can do which is also a smart thing to do and that is to start buying things for the baby way before the baby has arrived. Doing this will get you excited for the baby and in addition will be smart financially on your end because you have prepared yourself and bought things overtime for the baby. Keep in mind while shopping for the baby you want to be smart and use your funds wisely. For example there will be plenty of gifts that you will receive at the baby shower, which in some cases have the baby covered most of their first year. You will also receive a lot of hand me downs from friends and families as well. To be safe I would purchase: bottles as for the first couple months of the baby life they will be eating and drinking out of one, and any mother would tell you that they are hard to clean and it can be tiring so to have a few extra bottles will not hurt - diapers as you will also receive more than enough diapers at the baby shower but you can never have to many diapers. Depending on how fast you get them potty trained they will be using diapers for the next two to three years. Keep in mind if your child outgrows a diaper size you can always exchange it for another size without having the receipt - purchasing something fun like a toy or a cool swing always help you to get excited for the baby arrival - purchasing matching outfits or a dad shirt for yourself can also start that bond - creating a fun baby room can also be fun but challenging, the challenging part would be battling with the mother on what the room would look like. The examples that I just shared are ways to get you excited and build that bond with the child before he/she is born but they do require you to spend money. Other ways of building a bond with your unborn child that does not require money are: taking plenty of photos throughout the pregnancy - attend doctor visits as it is something about monitoring the baby growth and hearing the heartbeat that makes the moment surreal - spending a lot of time with the mother and catering to her needs while she is pregnant, doing this puts you in an early role of being a provider and protector for your family which gets you more excited because you are ready for your child to witness how a man and father should act in regards to his family - falling more and more in love with the mother also helps to build that bond with your unborn child as it will also help maintain that bond throughout the child's life. Unfortunately when the mother and father are no longer together or in love, the father tends to break up with the child as well. Scholars, this should not be and we will discuss more about this in the section title "Breaking up with the Mother and not the Child"

So, we have built that bond with our unborn child but now we must continue to build on that bond. It is important to continue to build on that bond because during the first year or two of our child's life, as fathers we can stray away from our father duties and no longer work to build that bond. The first two or three years of the child life can be one of the most "boring" and hardest years of your life as a father in regards to building that bond. Since it can be hard and boring as fathers we tend not be as active in the child's life and kind of slip away in the background. Not being active in the child's life equals to not building a bond with that child. I understand that being a father around this time can be boring and hard, but that boring and hard time being spent with the child is what helps build that bond. In addition to that it helps create those precious memories that you will miss out on. Be patient I promise the fun times will come sooner than you know it. One day you are going to look up and your child is not going to want to spend as much time with you nor will they have the time, so just hold on to those moments while you can. Another reason why you should spend time with your child because it might sound kind of crazy, but when you start to spend a lot of time around someone you actually start to miss that person. Spending time with your child allows you to start missing them because they become apart of your daily routine. You cannot miss anyone that you do not spend time with. A perfect example of this would be my eighty year old grandmother. We say it all the time that she is too old to be watching kids and she knows it which is why she no longer watches kids. Though when it comes to my youngest son that is a different story.

When my grandmother goes without seeing him for a while she begins to call us asking about him and wondering when will he be back. There have been times when we were out of town for several days and needed someone to watch our son. We would normally ask her to keep him for one day and let someone else keep him for the remainder of the days we are gone. We would ask her to keep him for one day because we do not want to put so much stress on her, but instead she'll ask us why she cannot she keep him longer. The point I am making here is when you actually spend time with someone, you actually begin to miss them and want to spend more time with that person. My eighty year old grandmother who has already stated she is no longer watching kids due to her age, continues to only watch my son because of the bond they have created. If my grandmother who has raised all her kids can still create bonds and have the desire to want to spend time with kids, then as a father you surely can create a bond and have the desire to want to spend time with your child.

7

HAVING CHILDREN THAT YOU CANNOT SUPPORT

As your freshman year in majoring in fatherhood I think it is important to talk about this before it is to late. Whether you are a father of one child or aspiring to be a father, it is important to keep in mind that you should only have children that you can afford. Not only should you have children that you can afford, but you should also be able to give each and every one of your children the best in life and not just the minimum. What upsets me is when I witness myself and others go on family or church trips with other family or church members, but that one family does not attend the events due to not being able to finance themselves and their kids. Though they are unable to attend any events they continue to have more children. I do not understand how you allow your children to miss out on events and miss the opportunity to experience nice things in life because you cannot finance all your kids, but yet you continue to have more kids which makes it even harder to do anything for your family. It is not fair to your kids that they have to miss out on basic and memorable childhood memories because you decided to have several kids that you can barely support. Do not get my message confused with saying that your kids should be spoiled. That is not what I am saying here but what I am saying is that your child should not be fourteen years old and still have yet to experience going to six flags or a restaurant where you sit down and have a waiter who serves you. Sadly enough this happens because going to six flags or eating out at a restaurant will easily cost you over two hundred dollars because of the amount of kids you have to pay for. I personally would like to have more kids but the number one thing that is holding me back is finance. I wish that I can give my kids more now but unfortunately I cannot due to my income. I know having another child will make it even harder to provide and maintain the lifestyle I would like them to live. This is not to say that I am living in poverty or my family is struggling, but what I am saying is I wish I could provide a little more for my children and provide them with more opportunities to be successful. Though if I continue to stay at the financial level I am at now, I can still thank God for allowing me to provide for my family the way I have been able to provide. I know because of him my children do not want or have a need for anything. Sometimes I can get in my feelings and desire so strongly to have another child, but I begin to think about the goals that I have for my children and how they are difficult to reach right now. I know that having another child will be another financial responsibility and will make it even harder to reach the goals that I have for my children. In conclusion, what I am simply saying is do not have children that you cannot afford. I understand your love and desire to have more kids, but we must also keep in mind what it takes to raise a child and the financial responsibility it takes. One must put away their personal desire and think about what would be in the best interest of your family and child that you plan to bring into this world. Each case is a case by case decision but again one must consider all factors before making that decision on whether or not they decide to bring another child into this world.

    I was talking to a friend of mines and I was sharing with him how I would like to have more kids but the way my finances are set up I would not be able to provide the best for all my children. He mentioned that my thinking is similar to his motto and I want to share it with you. He stated the more kids you have the more you take away from the ones you already have. So fathers keep that statement in mind when you decide to have more kids. If having another child takes away from the children you already have, then it may not be a good idea to have another one at that time.

8

COLLEGE DAD

Being a college dad is really not that hard, at least not that hard for the dad. While the dad is off in college doing his own thing, the mother or grandparents is taking on the burden of caring for the child. As I mentioned earlier I was a college dad and was only a sophomore in college when my first son was born. As a dad in college I did it all wrong for the most part. There may have been a few things I did right but overall I could have been a better college dad. The first thing you need to do as a college dad is get you a job. Whether you work throughout the school year or only on weekends and throughout the school breaks. The point is you need to have some type of income so that you can help to provide for your child. I advise you to get a job before the baby is born so that you may get a head start on purchasing things for the baby as this will help take some burden off of you when the baby arrives. The next thing the college dad should do is buy the baby some diapers and wipes every paycheck. If you can afford to buy more which you should then buy the baby more than just diaper or wipes. You can even buy two boxes of diapers and wipes every paycheck. As a mother or whomever is taking care of your child while you are in college, it can be quite frustrating when they have to go to the store and spend their money every time the baby need something when you should be spending your money on the baby needs as well. Your parents did not have that baby and that mother did not have that baby on her own. You had that baby so it is your responsibility to care for that baby not your parents. Therefore, they should not be taking on the full financial responsibility of your baby. When I was in college my parents would tell me how it would be quite frustrating that they would have to spend their own money on my son. Do not get me wrong they did not mind providing for my son but they were just teaching me to be a responsible father, and how I need to provide for my son even while off in college. My mom would tell me that I know the baby will need diapers, therefore when I come home I should buy diapers for the baby or send money on a weekly basis. It was not that I was not providing for my son financially but it was the simple fact that my parents would have to call me and ask for money or would have to spend their own money because it was an immediate need. Scholars, this should not be because as a father we should be fully aware of our baby needs even while off in college. In order to prevent your parents or the mother from being frustrated, send money and baby needs every paycheck or on a weekly basis if you can. When you come home be sure that you are observant and see if there is something that the baby needs without someone having to ask you to get it. I understand you are in college so that you may provide a better life for your child, but you still have a financial responsibility that must not be neglected. I believe as college dads and dads in general we have the mindset that if no one ask then the baby must not need anything. We must not have this mindset and be proactive on meeting the needs of our child. The mother should not have to tell you what is needed as we should began to know by now because we are majoring in fatherhood. Also as a college dad you have to sacrifice some weekends and school breaks to spend time with your child. Whether it may be you go back home and spend time with your baby or you bring the baby back to school with you. Either one is fine all that matter is that you are spending time and taking care of your baby. Let me give you a little hint when it comes to taking your baby to school, college girls love babies so it will not be hard for you to take care of your baby while back in school because you will have plenty of help from your colleagues.

I want to reiterate this to my college dads. DO NOT use college as a way to run away from your responsibilities as a father and be sure you are in college taking care of business, meaning you need to make sure you graduate. Your family held you down and supported you while you were in college, therefore it is only right that you take care of business and you do what you are supposed to do. Your family did not support you while you were in college so that you can go off to college and mess around. They supported you so that you can get an education in order to provide a better life for you and your family.

So now that you have graduated from college what do you think should happen next. Yes of course you go back home and take on more responsibilities of being a dad, but now it is your turn to support the mother in her goals and dreams. What this means is that it is your turn to take on most of the burden of raising your child while you support the mother in her goals. If the mother's desire is to return back to school or have other goals that she would like to achieve, then as the father you must support her like she supported you while you were in college. I remember when I finished school I extended the invitation to my son's mother to return back to school while I take on most of the burden of raising our son. Why did I extend the invitation, because I wanted to support her in the same way she supported me when I was in college.

Junior

9

INCARCERATED FATHER

As many of you may know I was an incarcerated father, and for those of you who do not know I really was not an incarcerated father but at the same time I really was. Did I just confuse you? Ok let me explain for the ones I confused and who do not know my background of being incarcerated. I spent sixty days in Fulton County Jail in Atlanta, Georgia. Fulton County is the same jail where Gucci Mane, T.I, Lil Wayne, Katt Williams, Left Eye, and several other celebrities were booked and served their time of being incarcerated. I also was booked and served time in that same exact jail. The biggest difference in my time of being incarcerated and the celebrities I just mentioned is that I committed no crime and voluntarily chose to be an inmate. Yes, you heard me correct. I voluntarily gave up my freedom to become an inmate of Fulton County. Though I was an inmate I was not just any type of inmate. I was an undercover inmate of Fulton County and the only person who knew that I was undercover was the chief jailer. No I was not a snitch as everything I did as an inmate was documented and aired on national tv. Lets just say it was more so of a research that I conducted. While being incarcerated I expected to learn and grow in a lot of areas, but one area that I surprisingly learned and grew in was being a father. Being incarcerated allowed me to miss the role of being a father and it also allowed me to get an insight on the impact of having fathers who have not majored in fatherhood. During my time in Fulton County there appeared to be a pattern. I would ask a lot of the inmates about their relationship with their father and about ninety percent of the inmates had little to no relationship with their father. In some cases the inmates father were also locked up and to go even deeper than that, some of the inmates father were locked up in Fulton County serving time along with their sons. Yes, you heard me correct it was almost like a family reunion. This is why it is important that we major in fatherhood but beyond majoring in fatherhood, we must also receive our degree in fatherhood as well. If more fathers majored in fatherhood I can rest assure that the jails would be less crowded and the expectations for fathers and males in general would rise. As we know the standard and expectations for fathers are very low so let's come together and put in the work that is needed so we can raise those expectations.

Another reason why it is important for us fathers to prevent from being incarcerated is due to fact that it is unfair to our children. When a father is incarcerated not only is he affected by this but everyone who is associated with the father is also affected. In particular the children and mothers are the ones who are most affected by this action. Remember I am speaking from experience as most of my thoughts in this book is based on experience or data. A mother is affected by the father's incarceration because now she has become the sole provider for your children. With the father being incarcerated her home just went from a two household income to a one household income overnight. As a father you have just put more responsibility on the mother to take care of the home and depending on her income this may not be a task that she is not quite ready for. Even if the father and mother do not live together and she has always only had one income, she will still lose that financial support from you because you will be incarcerated and unable to work and provide for your children. Due to your decision to be incarcerated you have now put your children at risk financially and you have also put the pressure on other family members to step up financially.

Your children do not deserve this because you have made the decision to not follow the law. I remember when I was incarcerated my wife would tell me how she was going broke because every week she was putting money on our daughter's lunch account and then would turn right around and put money on my books. Granted the production company was giving her money to put on my books, but items are high in jail and what they were giving her was not enough for me. So we were pretty much going into our own accounts to finance me while I was incarcerated. Fortunate for me I had income coming in so this was not a burden on me and my family, but I can imagine the burden it can have on fathers who are incarcerated. The inmates I met were losing their cars and homes due to not being able to make payments. If the children and mothers of these inmates were depending on the father's income and transportation, then these families were in trouble and I have witnessed the fathers stress over the fact that their family has to try and adjust their whole life. The sad part about the situation is that the father's have no control over the situation.

    Your children are also affected by you being incarcerated because everything we have and will talk about in this book, you will not be able to apply due to your incarceration. As an incarcerated father you will miss out on a lot of key and major events of your child's life. Depending on when and how long you will be incarcerated you may miss out on birthdays, first day of school, sporting events, prom, graduation, and the list goes on. The unfortunate part about this is you will never be able to get this time back. As we know time waits for no one and you can never get time back. Once your child take that first step or that beautiful walk up the aisle, you will never be able to go back in time and capture that beautiful moment. For me personally I missed my kids first day of school and birthday while incarcerated and that was enough for me. Kids grow so fast so when I was released and was finally able to be reunited with them, it felt as if I missed out on a lot of moments in their life. Before being incarcerated my two year old son went from speaking broken English to speaking in short and complete sentences just that fast. No matter how long you are incarcerated you will surely miss a milestone in your child's life.

I want to speak from a personal viewpoint on incarcerated fathers real quick. Obviously in jail you cannot really trust anyone and everyone has their own way of feeling the inmate out. For me I would ask the inmate about their relationship with their children. The inmate's answer would tell me a lot about that person and it would help me to determine the type of relationship I should have with that person moving forward. My perception was if you can treat your kids any kind of way then how can I trust and hold you to a high expectation with our relationship especially while being locked up. You do not care about your children in the free world so no telling how you will treat me in this hostile environment.

In conclusion, what I would like for you to take from this section is: Being an incarcerated father will hinder you from majoring in fatherhood. Being incarcerated means there will be less opportunities for young men to major in fatherhood.

My time of being in incarcerated I noticed that majority of the men that are incarcerated did not have a father who majored in fatherhood, and majority of men who are not incarcerated did have father who majored in fatherhood. Being incarcerated affects your children and it is not fair to your children.

10

Lifetime Commitment

Being a father is a lifetime commitment. Do not believe that since your children are growing or have become adults that your father duties are over with. Yes, you have less responsibilities and you no longer have to provide for them, but there are some duties that you must continue to do as a father. One way we know that we have majored in fatherhood throughout our child's life is when your child continues to look to you for advice and confirmation even as an adult. I remember talking with my great-grandfather and he mentioned to me how him and my grandfather's relationship had not been so great over the past years. One of the things that he mentioned was that my grandfather no longer calls him for advice or when he makes major decisions. When he first mentioned it to me I thought to myself that it was not a big deal and wondered why would he make mention of his son no longer calling him for advice. My great-grandfather went on to say how as an adult you should still call your father and ask him for advice. As I sat and let his statement process it began to make sense. I thought about how even as an adult I continue to call my father for advice. When I made the decision to buy a home, get married, or any problems that I may have within my family I would always look to my dad for advice. I may have not always took his advice but I looked to him for advice and would take it into consideration. Why do you think that as an adult I continue to look to my father for advice? I continued to look to my father for advice because my father majored in fatherhood. With my father majoring in fatherhood I knew that he had the experience and knowledge to advise me on what to do as a father and a man. Majoring in fatherhood does not only mean you have the skills and knowledge to be an excellent father, but it also means you have the skills and knowledge to be an excellent man. Fatherhood is apart of manhood and manhood is apart of fatherhood, you cannot be a father without being a man and you cannot be a man without being a father. As a father you have a lifetime commitment of advising and leading your child to success, and by doing so you know that you have majored in fatherhood.

Keep in mind as a father we will continue to give advice to our adult children, but it is important that as fathers we are ready to be an example and give a lifetime of helpful advice about relationships. Whether your daughter is dating or married she will continue to ask you for advice and will look to you for help when she is in trouble with her significant other. As we know man can really take a toll on woman, and we do not want our daughters to be the one that these men are abusing and misusing. This is why it is important that you major in fatherhood, because if you do not your daughter will see it and it will be hard for you to advise her. At the same time while it will be hard for you to advise her, it will also be hard for your daughter to receive your advice. When giving your daughter advice she will say to herself what do you know about being a good father or good to women when you were neither a good father nor a good husband. It will be hard for your daughter to receive advice from you, and unfortunately you may see your daughter experience a lot of hardship in her love life due to you not majoring in fatherhood. This is why it is important to follow the advice in this book and be an example to your children.

Another life time commitment that you may have to commit to as a father is a financial commitment. A financial commitment does not mean that you are still financing them on a day to day basis, rather financing them when they are in financial trouble. Examples of financial trouble are loss of job, not budgeting appropriately, or simply being uneducated on the economy and how it works. I recall one time a friend of mines came across a lump sum of money. She took $10,000 of that lump sum and put it towards her car thinking that she would have it paid up for the next year or so. About three months later she received a letter stating that her car would be towed if she did not make a payment as she was three months behind on her car payment. She was unaware that the $10,000 that was applied to her car note was applied to the principal and not applied to the payments over the next several months. Being uninformed on how her payments and loan worked she was only a few days away from having her car repoed, and was unable to make the payments due to believing that her car payments was something that she would not have to worry about over the next year or so. Her parents had to come together and support her with her car note over the next few months until she was able to make the proper adjustments and start back paying her car note on her own. This is a perfect example of our children getting in financial trouble and as fathers we still have a lifetime of financial commitment to our children. My friend was being a responsible adult by believing that she was making payments on her car note, but only in the end to find out that her payments were not being applied monthly. She must now find a way to make payments on her car before being repoed. As a parent and father we must support our child who was being responsible but made a financial mistake in the process. This is only one of the many ways our adult children may get in financial trouble. I can probably write a few chapters on how much financial trouble our children can get into but I will not do that. Just know that when you tell yourself you cannot wait until your kids turn eighteen so they can be out your pockets, that they will always find a way back in your pockets. Again, prepare yourself for the financial commitment to your children even after they turn eighteen. At the same time keep in mind if you have done everything that you were supposed to do in regards to raising your children, when you get old your children will have a financial commitment to you that they must and will fulfill.

11
A Bullying Mother

As fathers, we cannot allow the mother to bully us. In a marriage, I probably would not call it bullying, but it would be more like a dog fight and the father just so happens to lose most of the time. In a co-parenting relationship the mother and father can tend to bully one another. In this section, I want to mainly focus on the mother being a bully and as a father how one should handle the situation.

Often times when a mother does not get her way in regards to decision making for the child, she will start making demands and threats as opposed to just coming to an agreement or agreeing to disagree. The mother may demand the father to do something for her or the child without having any discussion or background on the father situation. Not only will she demand it, but her demeanor may come off as "I wish you would have something to say about it" or a Stone Cold Steve Austin type of attitude and say " that is the bottom line cause Stone Cold Steve Austin said so". Dealing with these individuals can be tough especially when the attitude is not necessary. The first thing you want to do is explain to her that the approach is not necessary as she should know your track record by now and should know that you will provide what is necessary for your child. I know in some situations you cannot say this because the mother will just find anything to argue about. If this is you then do not even acknowledge her attitude and just carry on with what is needed or what is not needed. Whatever you decide to do' do it because it is in the best interest of the child and not because the mother has made you feel that you must do it. Remember you are a student of fatherhood and you also know what is in the best interest of the child, and you also know when the mother knows what is best for the child. So whatever decision you make do not base it solely on the mother's demand but on what is in the best interest of the child and within reason. Another way a mother will try to bully you is by making threats. This may be the toughest and hardest type of bullying to deal with. The mother threats can affect so much of your personal life to your finances, career, and current marriage and/or relationship. I mean after all you do have history with her and she probably knows more about you than she should. Nevertheless, whatever you do you must not allow the mother to control you with her threats. A mother controlling you with her threats is like satan trying to control your life with threats. I am not calling the mother of your child satan, but you know how sometimes satan try to make threats on your life so you will not succeed or fulfill God's will. Well that is how it can feel when the mother makes threats on your life. The mother will tell you how she will begin to do this and that to make your life hell, but you cannot allow her to have that kind of power or influence over your life. As a father you must make a decision on what is in the best interest of the child, and not solely based on your thoughts or threats by the mother. I can understand you may not want the mother to fulfill those threats, but you also cannot allow the mother to control your life or happiness with threats. As a father and your professor throughout your studies of fatherhood I will never tell another father to allow the mother to bully him, but at the same time one must know how to humble himself and as the saying goes pick and choose your battles.

Throughout this course I discussed about how we should start a family the right way which is the biblical way. I explained that having a family the biblical way can eliminate a lot of problems and one of those problems are blended family problems. In a blended family the mother demands and threats can affect your marriage, but as fathers we must not allow this to happen. As I mentioned earlier being a father of kids in two different homes is one of the hardest things for me to do as a father and the mothers have no idea how hard it is for me. As a father sometimes the mother will make demands or requests that you may not be able to fulfill due to certain circumstances in your home. Being unaware of your situation telling her that I cannot or I do not have is not good enough for her. Now you are stuck between having to deal with: the angry mother because you are unable to provide for something at the moment - not really wanting to tell her why you are unable to provide in respect to the privacy of your home and marriage - having to deal with the threats of the mother - and now dealing with an upset wife because of the threats and drama that has been brought on to you. You are now in a tough situation, but nevertheless you cannot allow the mother's threats to effect your marriage and home. If you are doing what you are supposed to be doing as a father and have majored in fatherhood, then you have nothing to worry about and the mother's threats and demands cannot and will not affect you.

Mothers, I also understand that you do not want to bully the father but just simply want to hold him accountable. As you hold him accountable you must be sure that you are not doing so in a bullying manner. Sometimes we need you to hold us accountable and help teach us on how to be a father but bullying us will not help. So for my mothers I need you to keep in mind when speaking with the fathers and trying to hold them accountable, that it is not in a bullying manner because a bully only makes things worse.

The message that I would like for you to take out of this section is to not allow the mother of your child to bully or control your life with threats and demands. Again this can all be avoided if handled the biblical way and waiting until marriage to have sex and start a family.

12

Child Support

Child support is probably every man's nightmare and is something that you almost cannot avoid especially if you have a mother who is a bully. I think we all know what child support is but in case you do not know, child support is when one parent is required to pay the other parent an amount that is determined by the state guidelines. The money that is payed to the parent is used to support the children they have together. There are so many dynamics to the child support policy and child support will not only affect the family that is involved but it can also affect society as a whole. In some cases child support can be effective but research has shown that child support is not effective nor is it effective in the way it is intended for. I probably lost my mothers on this one but just stay with me here. I like to say that the child support policy built the road with good intentions to hell. Meaning when lawmakers created the child support policy it was made with good intentions but the good intentions only lead the pathway to hell. In this section I will give a brief history, social problem, goal, target population, funding, and effectiveness in the child support policy. Also below are terms that will be used throughout this section that you must be familiar with:

Custodial parent - A parent who is given physical or legal custody by the courts. This parent is normally the person that the child lives with and makes all the legal decisions for the child.
Non-custodial parent - A parent who the child does not live with nor is not given legal custody of the child. This parent is the one normally paying child support.

Child support became a policy in 1975 and the policy was supported by the federal and state government. Since then congress has revised the child support policy several times. When child support was first implemented it was the non-custodial parent's responsibility to send payments to custodial parent. It was not until about 1990 when a new approach was implemented and that approach was the government garnishing the wages of the non-custodial parent. Since then other government assistance programs have backed up the child support policy. Other government assistance programs such as the food stamp office, Women Infant Children (WIC), and Temporary Assistance for Needy Families (TANF) along with other agencies have all supported the child support policy. These agencies have supported the child support policy by no longer providing assistance to parents who do not have the non-custodial parent on child support. If a custodial parent wishes to receive government assistance he/she must first put the non-custodial parent on child support. If the non-custodial parent is not on child support the agency will assist the custodial parent in opening up a case. The custodial parent must be cooperative in locating the non-custodial parent and putting him on child support. Once child support is put into place the custodial parent will then be able to receive government assistance. In some cases once the child support is put into place the custodial parent may not be eligible for government assistance. The reason for this is once the custodial parent begins to receive monthly payments of child support, the custodial parent income has just increased and the income may be too high to qualify for certain government assistance. So fathers be aware that in some cases the mother is not putting you on child support with evil intentions, but she is forced to in order to receive the support and resources that is needed to support your child.

The goal of the child support policy is to provide financial assistance to children who parents have separated or is not married. The funds from child support should be used for utilities, housing, day to day needs and entertainment. All which is for the well being and support of the children. The problem is in most cases the goal is not being met, and others are benefiting more from the child support policy when in fact the child should be the one benefiting from the policy. When I ask someone who do they think benefits most from child support, what do you believe to be the number one answer? Yes, you guessed it right, everyone believes that the mother benefits the most from child support. In fact the mother and the child are at the bottom of the list and the people who benefit the most from child support are the individuals who helps to enforce the child support policy. These individual includes: attorneys - court systems which consist of judges, boards, and division - law enforcements - and bureau of prisons. These individuals benefit the most from child support policy and not the child, and let's not forget the policy was intended to benefit the children and family. You ask how are the individuals who are enforcing the policy benefiting from the child support policy ….. easy! It is probably not a surprise that we have more individuals that are behind on child support or is simply not paying their child support as opposed to individuals who are. It is reported that the overwhelming number of non-custodial fathers that are not on child support orders who qualifies for child support could owe as much as thirty-four billion in unpaid child support. There are billions in child support that goes unpaid in the U.S each year, and as a result innocent families are forced into poverty. For those individuals that are not paying into child support, those individuals must be punished or located for not paying child support and the government must hire individuals to punish and locate the individuals who choose to disobey the law. For example: the judge is paid to sign off on the warrant or hear the case on why the non-custodial parent has not been located - the constable is paid to locate and serve the non-custodial parent - a police officer is paid to locate the non-custodial parent and arrest him on unpaid child support - and an attorney is paid to represent the non-custodial parent and child. It was reported that the average attorney makes about $15,589 for a child support case and the civil court makes about $10,765. The agency that benefits the most from child support policy would be the Bureau of Prisons. Payroll shows that the prison makes about $1,128,362 from individuals who are incarcerated due to the child support policy. While all these individuals are being paid to enforce the child support policy, the child has yet to be paid and benefit from the policy. Over millions of dollars are being paid out to enforce the policy, and not even half of what is being paid to enforce the policy is actually being paid into child support. In the end not only does the child not benefit the most from the policy, but taxpayers are also suffering from this policy. With all this said I am not saying that all families and children are not benefiting from the child support policy, but they are the ones to least benefit from the policy and these are the individuals who should be benefiting the most from the policy. I am sure in some homes children and families are benefiting from what the policy is intended for, but in most homes children and families are certainly not making the most of the policy. This is why I say the road was built with good intentions to hell. Law makers created this policy hoping to support families and prevent families from falling into poverty which I believe is good intentions on the law makers part, but the cost to enforce the policy, poor policy implementation, and the many individuals who have chosen to not follow the law have made this policy difficult to reach its ultimate goal and in the end our children suffer.

There are other social problems associated with child support outside of the child not benefiting from the policy and the effect it has on taxpayers money and that is incarceration. As a non-custodial parent who fails to maintain his financial responsibility and not pay his child support, as a result of their non-payment they risk being incarcerated. If incarcerated, the custodial parent may become the sole financial provider for the child, and the government has just removed the little help the mother did have. While incarcerated the non-custodial parent is unable to perform the appropriate duties for their child(ren), and may hinder the relationship because of time loss due to their incarceration. Research also shows how child support can hinder a father-child relationship, but I want us fathers to change our way of thinking and the research. Research shows that the more a father pays into child support the less time a father will spend with their child. The non-custodial father feels that the child support payment compensate the visits. Remember throughout your freshman, sophomore, and junior year I taught you that we cannot substitute time for money. Rather the money is given voluntarily or involuntarily we cannot substitute time for money. As fathers we have to get out of the mindset of thinking that our money makes it ok to spend less time with our children. In some cases spending more money in child support can naturally result in less time with your child which brings me to our next social problem. High payments in child support can make the father feel that he needs to make up for lost income. A result of this will cause the father to increase his time in the workforce which will result in reducing his time with the child. This can also backfire and leaving the father with no desire to earn more income or becoming financially stable because the father knows that the more he makes the more he has to pay in child support, and he is unable to enjoy the fruits of his labor. Paying more in child support brings me to my next social problem and that is the adequate amount of support that is paid to the custodial parent. A problem that the parents may face during the child support process will be are the payments to small which could still leave the child basic needs to not be met or will the non-custodial parent pay to much in child support which can take away from the non-custodial home and basic needs of children living in his home. As we can see lawmakers have yet put into place the perfect formula to assure that the child needs is being met while at the same time assuring that the father and his family needs are being met as well. I know in the state of Texas if you're caring for other children your child support payments will be reduced.

    We have also learned the effectiveness of the child support policy is only effective to a small portion of the intended population but it is not effective to the overall intended population. This is why I highly encourage both the mother and father to come to an agreement outside of court, because I can almost guarantee that neither the mother nor father will be 100% satisfied with the decision that the judge makes. Another reason you should avoid going to court because what this does is enter a legal war. In the war both parents will encounter financial loss. Financial losses include but are not limited to: legal fees, court costs, and time off work. Also in this war both parents are often times so caught up into winning that they forget that the reason they are in court is for the well being of their child. Again, I highly encourage both the mother and father to settle payments and visitation outside of court. The custodial parent can still have payments garnished through the attorney general without having to appear before the judge. This makes it easier for both parties and can put the custodial parent at ease knowing that she will receive payments for child support without having to appear before a judge. Mothers keep in mind that the child support policy was originally created for absent fathers and not failed relationships or because the father has made you upset. Remember that the policy is ineffective so let's work together to make the policy effective. Fathers, you too must also do your part in supporting the child and cooperating with the system to avoid any other damages that the policy has already caused to society. In the end I know that paying child support may be a burden at times, but at the end of the day the funds are being used to help the well being of your child and the mother whom is taking care of your child.

And for the record I am not stating that I am for child support nor am I stating that I am against child support. It is really a case by case situation as the goal of child support is to keep single parent families out of poverty and to hold the non-custodial parent accountable for their child.

Senior

13

No Excuses

Scholars, we must no longer give excuses on why we cannot do or why we cannot see our children. Again, I am not faulting fathers who have made excuses as I was once was a father who made excuses.

I never realized I made excuses to not see or do for my children until I witnessed others make excuses on not caring for their children. I can recall this happening on two occasions, the first occasion occurred when I heard a young man make excuses on why he cannot see or care for his daughter. He would make so many lousy excuses on why he could not perform his fatherly duties it was ridiculous and even as a father myself who had not majored in fatherhood could see how pathetic his excuses were. When I first heard the excuses I thought to myself on how sorry and lazy of a father he was. Then as time went on I thought to myself how lazy I might have been in the past because some of the excuses he has used I too have used within my journey of fatherhood. Of course this was before I had majored in fatherhood but the point is I still used these excuses with having no knowledge on what type of commitment it really took to raise a child. At the time when I used the excuses I thought they were legit excuses, but now I know they were just what they were and that is excuses. The sad part about the situation is the things that I were making excuses for were things that are part of being a father, but now I am well aware that it is all part of being a father and no more excuses. The second occasion occurred when I was incarcerated at Fulton County Jail. During my time in Fulton County one of my roommates was released from Fulton County. About a week later he had returned back to Fulton County of course it broke my heart to see him return especially after he told me that he had spent more time being locked up than being in the free world and he was only twenty years old. I had a chance to talk with him when he had returned and I asked him what did he do with his short time of being a free man. He shared with me the things he did while he was out and he also mentioned that his son had a birthday while he was out. I then asked him what did he do for his son on his birthday and he shared with my that he did not see his son on his birthday. I then proceeded to ask him why did he not spend anytime with his son while he was released. He stated to me that he did not have a ride and plus it was to far of a drive to go see his son. I immediately thought to myself wow that used to be me, I use to say things like my son was to far or if the mother cannot meet me then I will not get him because it is to far of a drive for me. Obviously you cannot really compare my situation to the inmate, because as he mentioned he been locked up most of his life and his son life so every opportunity he got he should have used it to spend time with his son. In my situation I was off in college or lived an hour away from my son so every opportunity I got I should have been using it to spend time with my son as opposed to thinking that I have a two hour round trip which makes four hours all together just to spend one day with my son. At the time I just thought it was not worth it but now I know that it is absolutely worth it, especially if you do not see your child on a weekly basis. Again I cannot fault neither young man for thinking the way they were thinking because those were once my thoughts and sometimes it takes you looking in from the outside to change your perspective. I now know that is not the right mindset to have and it is my job to educate the fathers on no more excuses. I did inform the young man in jail that it probably would have been a good idea to go visit his son, but I did not push the issue because for one it was sort of to late and secondly I was trying to keep a low profile so I could not really press the issue to much on how someone needs to be spending time with their children when I too was incarcerated and not spending time with my children. I have not yet to inform the other young man on his excuses that he has made in the past or may still make because it is not my place to teach and educate him. Yes, I would like to but again it is not my place and he may not be receptive to the knowledge and advice I have for him as a father and as a man. No disrespect to him as a father as I have seen him grow as a father but I do believe he still has a lot of room to grow as he is still one of those every other weekend fathers we talked about and may be just performing a little above minimum. Remember fathers we are no longer every other weekend dads nor do we no longer do our jobs at a minimum. Who knows maybe the young man will purchase my book and may receive the information better from my book as opposed to me coming to him direct. Let this be a teaching moment when trying to coach someone on how to major in fatherhood. Every father you encounter will not take advice from you, it may take someone else to give him the advice as he would probably receive it better from someone else rather than receiving it from you. Its like sharing your religious beliefs with someone. You know you talk to someone about your god or religion for many years and they do not want to hear it or believe it, but someone else come along and talk to them for a day about the same religion and now they believe it. Not sure what they said or how they said it but they received it better from someone else as opposed to receiving it from you. that is how it is when coaching someone on being a father. That father may better receive the information from someone else, but know that when it is your time to empower a father you will have the tools to help them after reading this book.

Though I have made excuses in the past I want to be clear that I was never just a deadbeat father. I probably was not always the best father and lived up to my full potential, but I was also never a deadbeat father. I always supported and spent time with my son to a certain degree. Just wanted to make that clear for the record and did not want to confuse any of my readers.

14

BREAKING UP WITH THE MOTHER AND NOT THE CHILD

God forbid that things do not work out with you and the mother of your child. As you know I want nothing more than for things to work out between the two of you, and for you and your family to be one big happy family. Unfortunately, it does not always happen that way and it may require for you to part ways with the mother of your child. If this is the case then this section is for you and I will educate you on how to break up with the mother while continuing to be an active father. I have witnessed far too many times families breaking up and it is almost like as if when the father decided to break up with the mother he also decided to break up with the children. I know that you thought you and the mother were going to be together for a lifetime and it did not quite work out that way, but you and your children will definitely be together for a lifetime and there is no breaking up with them. Though, as fathers, we may be bitter or angry about the break up we cannot take that out on our children and lower our standards. We must continue to be active in our children's lives and not let the break up result in you being an "every other weekend dad" or even worse not being an active father at all.

Again, I understand you may be going through a lot because of the breakup or you may feel free and want to live life after the break up. Keep in mind you still have your commitment as a father and you are breaking up with the mother and not the children.

15

FATHER'S DAY

Father's Day is a day where we recognize and celebrate the fathers. To some this day may be known as "bash your irresponsible father day". On social media, I often post the day before Father's Day asking if we cannot bash the fathers on this day; stating how we do not care how sorry or how much you hate your baby daddy and/or father. We get it. Your father or the father of your child did not major in fatherhood and are not good fathers, but you should not take this celebration away from the good fathers.

It is quite funny because I normally have one person to comment under my post and say something along the line "well get ready because you know they coming and it is about to go down." Even my followers know that the bashing of the fathers is about to begin. You know what else bothers me on Father's Day? When a mother post a picture of herself on social media and the caption reads "Happy Father's Day to me." For one, you are not biologically the father, you may play the role of the father in your child's life but technically you are not the father. I am sure you play the role of the father and many other roles to your child but I do not see you posting on grandparents day or any other day talking about "Happy grandparents day to me". Just as silly as it may sound for you to say that it is just as silly for you to acknowledge yourself as a father on Father's Day. We see and know that your child has an absent father in their life and that is why we acknowledge you on Mothers day. Also because your child has an absent father in their life we do not call you a father but we refer to that as being a single mother and that is ok. I know plenty of single mothers who have raised excellent children, but as single mothers let's try to stay away from bashing fathers and let fathers have their day on Father's Day.

Fathers, we must do better overall as fathers so that we may take our day back and there will no longer be a need to bash the fathers. On Father's Day and even throughout the year, mothers will talk bad about fathers and you have people who will allow it to happen. It hurts me to see this because I am a father myself and I know what the hurt mothers are saying is not a representation of me or fathers as a whole. Fathers are just as important as mothers and we need to make society believe this as well. We are living in a day in time where mothers feel that their children do not need their father in their life. In reality, the child needs their mother and father in their life. Fathers, let's take back our day and be important to society again. My prayer is that the father community comes together and raise the standard of fathers along with coming together and uplifting one another as fathers and man.

Calvin Crosby IV

Finals

16

TRUTH OR SLANDER

Time to prep you for your final exam. I conducted a comprehensive study over the last few years collecting sentiment from parents, family members and spectators on their perspective on parenting. Here's a list of the top general conversation points when it comes to fatherhood.

When it is time for fathers to watch their children is this called babysitting?

Slander. How can we babysit our children? When a mother is watching her children people do not call it babysitting so why is it when a father is watching his children it is referred to as babysitting? A father cannot babysit his children and we must get out that mindset because a father should be caregiving for his children just as much as the mother.

Stay at home dads are lazy and weak.

Slander. Just because a father chooses to pursue being the full time stay at home parent does not mean he is weak. This only applies if that father is making the decision based on the best interest of the family. For example, the mother may have a demanding career that may require the father to be a full time dad or only work part time. If the mother's career is more successful and able to provide a better future for the family, then it may be in the best interest for the father to be a stay at home dad or find a job that allows him to do both while he supports the mother and her career. Supporting the mother in her career does not mean the father is weak or lazy. It means that he has humbled himself in order to provide a better future for him and his family.

Fathers believe that stay at home moms have it easy.

Truth. As fathers we think that stay at home moms have it easier. We believe that it is easier to focus on the home full time as opposed to getting up and going to work everyday. In fact being a stay at home mom can be harder and can also take a toll on the mother if she allows it to. It can be hard to be a stay at home mom and as a father you must support the mother, protecting her from possible physical exhaustion or mental breakdowns.

Calvin Crosby IV

End of the Semester

Take the Final and see how you score

17
THE FINAL

As a father we only need to see our children every other weekend or standard visitation

- ❏ True
- ❏ False

2. Child support is the best solution for you, your family, and the child

- ❏ True
- ❏ False

3. The child support policy is effective overall

- ❏ True
- ❏ False

4. Who benefits the most from child support?

    A. Mother

B. Child
C. Legal System
D. Father

5. When fathers watch their children this is considered babysitting

- ❏ True
- ❏ False

6. As a father should you make decisions solely based on the mother threats

- ❏ True
- ❏ False

7. It is ok to continue to have children because you know that one day your financial situation will get better

- ❏ True
- ❏ False

8. Fill in the blank:

The _____ children you have the _____ you take away from the _____ you already have.

9. Is parenting a 50/50 contribution

- ❏ True
- ❏ False

10. Who can major in fatherhood?

A. Only Fathers
B. Only Mothers
C. Everyone
D. Grandparents

Answers:
1. F 2. F 3. F 4. Legal System 5. F 6. F 7. F 8. more, more, children 9. F 10. everyone

18

Graduation Day

Congratulations, you have now graduated and received your degree in fatherhood. I am proud of you as you have endured and completed all the requirements to major in fatherhood. Know that not only am I proud of you for graduating but your family is also proud of you for stepping up and taking on the role of being a father. I know that it is not easy to be a father and apply the tools that you have been taught, but the community and your children need you and it is imperative that you apply those tool in order to be a better father and serve your community.

You should also be proud of yourself as I know that it was not easy taking time out your busy schedule to be with me and learn how to be a better father. I know that it took a lot of dedication, studying, and practice to get to where you are now. Understand that your hard work will not go overlooked and your children, whom you did this for, will one day appreciate you for this.

I remember when I was in college and one of my biggest inspirations to graduate was my son. I wanted my son to live a better life and more importantly all I wanted him to know was that daddy graduated from college and was a professional. Know that graduating before your son or daughter becomes a certain age, the only thing they will ever know is that you are an outstanding father. They will minimize the mistakes or struggles because you actively worked to resolve them. Please do not be hard on yourself and compare yourself to other fathers or feel that now you have graduated you will instantly become super dad. It will take time and practice but know that you will surely reach your full potential and be the best father you desire to be.

One last thing I want you to take away on your graduation day, as a father do not live to try to get the approval of others of being an excellent father. You may be living your whole life to gain the approval of others especially the mother of your child. You should now have the knowledge to know what it takes to be an excellent father. It is not about getting the approval of others, though confirmation from others is always good, but it is about carrying out the responsibility of a father to your child whether others think it is excellent or not. Again I say, *do thy duty that is best and leave unto the Lord the rest*. Congratulations and I hope to see you in our Master's program.

Majoring In Fatherhood

Calvin Crosby IV

ABOUT THE AUTHOR

Calvin Crosby IV is a Fort Worth, TX native. Upon graduation Calvin received his degree in Social Work from Texas Woman's University in 2013. He began his career as a social worker for Child Protective Service. While in the role of a social worker Calvin faced many challenges, but the challenges only intensified his desire to work with the youth and within the community. In 2016, he became a certified teacher and began to work in education, where he had the opportunity to strengthen his passion for youth. In 2018, he received his Masters in education administration. Recently, Calvin participated in the docu-series titled "60 Days In" which aired on A&E. In this program, Calvin volunteered to go to jail as an undercover inmate. What made his experience unique is while he has never committed a crime or spent time incarcerated, he volunteered his time and freedom, and took on the risk of being incarcerated. Though Calvin was innocent, he was treated in the manner in which inmates are treated daily while incarcerated, with no staff or other inmates aware of his actual status. After the release of his docu-series he has had the opportunity to speak at various institutions and community engagements. Most recently, Calvin appeared on the Steve Harvey Show, and has had other television and radio appearances as well. Calvin is also a proud member of the Omega Psi Phi Fraternity Incorporated.

Calvin Crosby IV

www.ingramcontent.com/pod-product-compliance
Lightning Source LLC
Chambersburg PA
CBHW020943090426
42736CB00010B/1242